The Heart of Me

A Poetic Journey

By

LaToya Bragg

Layout:	LaToya Bragg FM Robinson
Editor:	LaToya Bragg
Co Editor:	FM Robinson
Cover Design:	FM Robinson

Publisher License ID# A3M3G4XJ3F5SJ

Words From the Author

I have the heart of a giant and the Courage of a lion.
They want to shut me down but Look at how I Triumph

-Philly P

Dedication

This book I dedicate to my children, Katrina, Timothy, Michael and Dominique Bragg
Through all my (our) struggles You never stopped loving me as your mother. I love you all with all my heart
To my Mommy Denice Bragg and my future husband
Thank you all for your belief in me

Introduction

This is a five year time span of my favorite poetry I have written. These words were what my heart formed through the different situations I have lived. They are true expressions of me and what I was feeling during time frames.

Table of Contents

CHAPTER I
Gospels of My Soul

Table of Contents-Continued

CHAPTER I
The Gospels of My Soul

No Shame

I will not be ashamed of loving God
He is the One who made me who I are
He has always been there for me
My friend..I have never seen
He speaks a truth in my ear
That I wish the whole world could hear
He lifts me when I am down
Holds me when no one else is around
Keeps every promise that He makes
Love to real to ever be fake
Heart to big to be selfish
He calls me Princess..His precious
I wake up singing Him a song
Because to Him..I belong
No matter what the people say
I'm gonna trust You anyway
Gonna praise You anyway
You are my life and I can't let go
Even if they disagree
It don't even bother me
This ain't they life
I don't have to fuss and fight
I pray until I get it right
You are my light

Dear God

As I write these words that are so true
Take control of my life and do what You do
Worried night after night
Not the way I want to live life
Drinking Pepsi smoking cigarettes
Over days past..stressing
I can't begin to change
Guessing about a future that haven't even came
To shake my habitual ways
Knowing with You I have a life of favor
Plus the greatest love to gain
Month after month I'm going insane
Taking my time to please everybody else
I'm not even happy with myself
Then I ain't no fool
I know perfection comes from You
You are love, truth, peace and joy
Available to every girl and boy

Forgiven

The dreams I believe
The ones the world tried to take from me
My love, my writing, my creativity
Couldn't see the future You offer me
Its so overwhelming how You will renew me
Restore. Bless my friends and family
Forgive and cleanse me of my sins
Heal my brokenness from love lost men
Give me a life to start over again
I accept the One who has no beginning nor no end
Offer up my temple to the Holy Spirit
Will use for Your glory my spiritual gifts
I know I owe You me
Sent a savior so I can be free
I made the choices that put me at a disadvantage
Live destructively. You always clean up the damage
I've known this since I was eight
All it took was a little bit of faith
I've seen the miracles again and again
Especially in my life of sin
Time after time: forgiven
Welcomed in
Well this time God I want my feet planted solid
For You to put away the polish
Cause me to shine so bright
I can be seen in the darkest of nights
Because you see Lord I couldn't see me
But I could hear Your enemy
Mean, rude and loud
Telling me how everything was gonna fall about
Talking about You don't love me at all
And for years I believed
I forgot its job was to kill, steal and deceive
Then I thought why am I so special that you would even bother
Eureka!!, I got it. Because I am so special to my Father
If I didn't have such purpose
You probably would have been wordless

You tried to kill me, steal me, Nearly deceived me
Into not accepting I belong to a King
The Victorious One that reigns supreme

My Faith

One day somebody said to me you praise God when you get high
I replied Yea and they said that ain't right
It took a few months
But finally I ask Him
God does it offend Thee
That I talk to thee after I smoke weed
He replied I created you. Praise me always
Now God knows I don't want to smoke all my life
But until I quit it's alright
See, its stuff like that that can make a person feel their going to hell
I started getting blowed at the age of twelve
It was my way to escape my living hell
My Father
He knows me so well
It is your heart daughter that is good and true
And I have been forgiven you
I had yet to forgive myself
Let alone somebody else
So I continued my journey thru hell
Feeling like I was inside prison cells
Just like fate
Jesus met me at the gate
I've been came to save thee
Take my hand and walk with me
I want to show you some things
Tell you some thing, give you some things
And I said yes to my calling
No more stumbling, falling
I wear my crown proudly
My Father is a King
Your not waiting on Him, He's waiting on you
He has promises and gifts for you too
This is all from love
Now Ya know
I believe in a Spirit above
Not above the earth

The Kingdom is in you first
Not meant to offend or enrage
I pray for so much peace in our days
I am just being Latoya
And this is something I wanted to share with ya

Loving God

I will not be ashamed of Loving God
It is the One who made me who I are
Always been there for me
My Friend...Never physically seen
Speaks a truth in my ear
I wish the whole world could here
The Spirit lifts me when I am down
Holds me when no one else is around
Keeps every promise that It makes
Love to real to ever be fake
Heart to big to be selfish
I am princess..Its precious
I wake up singing Ywhw a song
To the Great Spirit I belong
Jehovah provides every strength
Without it I would have died from this
Uncontainable pain would have drove me insane
Somehow it contained in my brain
If it would have been unleashed
There would have been death in the streets
The sea was stormy
But the waves never over turned me
Before the sea drowned me
Spiritually I was given peace
Oh, I don't need y'all to believe
I trust my Spirit Being
It is the one who made promises
And I trust Yahweh to honor them
To love me in no others way
Why my love is here to stay
I love being in the Presence
Want it forever and forever
I love You loving on me
Giving me sweet grace and mercy
My soul is never thirsty
My spirit will never die

Just move on to loving the Spirit in the Sky

I, I, I

I feel a shifting in my atmosphere
I speak and the Lord hears
I disobey and He still answers when I pray
I know He has kept me into this day
I scream out, “God, Please hear my cry”
I start to shed happy tears from my eyes
I am not transformed yet
I have yet to be my best
I am a believer of His word
I am protected by His blood
I am never alone
I have a God, He is my home

God's Grace

On one of my recent expenditures
My Lord took me on an adventure
Then we stood on the edge of a cliff
I was a lil bit miffed
He know I don't like heights
But, Oooohh, what a sight
With my eyes I could see
The most beautiful blue calm sea
The Sun glorious shining
Owning all of the horizon
The storm was so far in the distance
If I hadn't squinted my eyes I would have missed it
I looked at MY figure of God and smiled
Okay, Lord, I like this calm
True story. So I just shook my head
And thought Lord, You're gonna do everything that You said

Rise and Shine

I'm gonna rise and shine
Soar with the birds in the sky
Take the Diamond out of the rough
Wipe me off and shine me up
Rub off the polish, it’s the final touch..

I dream so big I can't get enough
It ain't about the cars and stuff
But the people I love so much
I wish I could grab them in a bunch
Hold them and remove their crutch..

So much talent. Not down the drain
Secretly hidden behind our pain
Tragedy happens. Lives change
Some will never be the same
No give up. We have to much to gain..

I have something more than love and dope
Preciously I call it hope
It's the thing that helps me cope
Blindly through the dark I grope
I might stumble but I never let go of the rope..

One day my dream will be reality
Nightmares o far behind me
I have faith in what I cannot see
I trust and believe
In promises made by a King

Ode to My Father

The more I trust God
The quicker my problems get solved
Learning not to think with my human mind
Because my Father is so spiritually kind
Not one day has He failed me
Even when I didn't know how to believe
I didn't see it when I received it
Now I do and He moves so quick
I trust for reasons
Yes, Lord, this is my season
Naw I don't have my house or my husband yet
But My King is giving me the best
He said, "All your habits shall go"
Don't know when but this I know
"All my children shall speak in tongues and be saved"
My God, what an amazing grace!!!
He calls me, "Prophet, miracle worker and healer
There is a power in my praise to break chains and deliver"
Hallelujah, I praise everyday
I know Your on Your way
I trust a God, My Lord, our Father
Stress and anger, why even be bothered?
Jehovah's gonna work it all out
No need to doubt

Mercy, Mercy, Me

Since I was a child I was a survivor
Now I am a prayer warrior
Lived my life full of fear
Depression caused so many tears
Pain seared through my body and heart
I thought me and the darkness would never part
So many sleepless nights
Wishing everything would be alright
Not knowing they already were
My Father had already provided a cure
It took me years to learn
His love, mercy..didn't have to be earned
Taking time to get over my old self
Lord knows I need a lot of help
The conditions of who I used to be
Still have not completely ceased
But oh yes I can envision a different me
I just don't look only where my eyes can see

Sick and Tired

I have to trust in someone, other than myself
Look to the Spirit for help..

Thought I could do this own
I'm tired of my hearts sad song..

The aches I can't explain
Didn't know I could take so much pain..

I had so much restraint
My weakness proved my strength..

Didn't know how strong I would get
Until my Savior came and we met..

But the weight of the world on your shoulders
Will let you know something: you can move boulders..

No need to cry, be sad or worry
Stressing over people being sorry..

Upset about the needs of tomorrow
Wondering why love brings sorrow

Find your strength pull what you need from it
Look to your gifts there just might be some thing you missed..

Even though we get misused and abused
You gotta fight like your not gonna lose..

You gotta make a choice so choose
Walk around hurt and confused..

Pull up the covers and let 'em walk all over you
or get up from sleep and do what you gotta do..

Do you have a dream

Remember it and scream..

"Mountain get outta my way"
Like Montel Williams taught me to say

Requiem of a Life

I am not about my circumstances
I am about my praise
The enemy doesn't stand a chance
Against God and His Heavenly ways..

Fear no longer lives inside me
Darkness has a new light
Faith lets me breathe freely
My Fathers love is outta sight..

I can feel it all around
He makes my heart smile
His voice is the sweetest sound
Since I was a child..

Disobedient I used to be
Still He granted mercy and favor
The King has what He has for me
I didn't have to change my behavior..

I believed in Him to be my Deliverer
Gave a lil bit of my heart and time
Trusted Jehovah to be my Healer
I raise up praising Him like the Sun shines..

I wait..in His arms I rest
Because He is not done
Giving me His best
Life I felt over..has just begun

Words from the Lord

I felt you had turned your back and ordered my punishment
Then I read Romans 8: There is therefore now no condemnation..
I stopped thinking about Your judgment
I accepted Your engagement
You engage in spiritual war for me
With that which I cannot see
Engage in my conversations
Take my day and rearrange it
People convinced me I had to “get myself right”
Left me feeling ashamed every night
Guilt had my tears racking my body
Feeling less than human. A nobody
You know the words Lord, I have often spoken
“Why am I so broken?
What's wrong with me?
Tell me what I did to offend thee?”
I embarked on my own journey
Wanted to know God personally
I learned..You chose me to be special
And You have always been helpful
I saw so much of the bad
I looked right past my Dad
Then in 2013 You said, “Tell her.” to Your children
“You love me, saved me, ordained me and call me Friend”
Then because I had spent a life in disbelief of Your love for me
It took some years for me to even begin to believe
My eyes could not see and my mind couldn’t imagine
What they prophesied You said would happen
I have gotten prophesies all my life
Not me. That can't be right!
“Your gonna be a healer!” 'I can't even help myself'
“Your gonna write best selling books!” 'I haven't wrote one yet'
“God is gonna send you a husband!” 'No lord! Do you know how much humping I'm doing?'
“And I saw musical notes coming off your lips!” 'I don't know how to write music'

"A house is coming for you!" 'How? I don't have any money'
"The Lord has a call of greater glory that's on you!" 'You must be talking to someone else, honey'
"Michigan is where the Lord want's you to be!
Your career, Your husband are here!" 'Is he talking to me?'
"Your a diamond in the rough and God has been polishing you up!"
'Now I can be believe that much'
"He has placed in you a special sensitivity and understanding!"
'Now that! I can definitely believe'
"Even as you were worshiping I brought the answer. Look for it in three days!"
It came and I was amazed
Then like all the others..that dream had to fade
Back to my mind. I was enslaved
With all I had been thru, still going thru
None of that could be true
So why did I still have hope?
Year after year wanting it more and more?
Finally almost 2016 I want to believe
Yes! There is..a writer in me
I got the messages on the streets. From Pastors with heat!!!
Bishop Willie Thornton from over in the Ink
And everything else that was said in the churches in Michigan
In Ohio now but I'm going back again

Not About Me

Its not about me..
So not about me
The lungs I use to breathe
Nor the eyes I use to see
Not even the bed I use to sleep...

Not the clothes I put on
Or the way my hair is done
So not about how I have my fun
Or when or where my car runs...

Its not about the legs I use to walk
And the mouth I use to talk
Too laugh, too kiss to eat
This
So not about me...

Not about the blood that courses thru my veins
Nor the body that brings me pain
Or the mind that wants to go insane
The Sun that shines after the rain...

The cigarettes that make me choke
The weed I hate to love to smoke
The impurities I want to go
So much more this I know..

It's not about those that called me names
Not people who played games
Things that brought me to shame
But a love I can explain...

See its not about the voices in my head
The heart that has bled
The times I wished I was dead
So my Heavenly Father says...
This is not about you

The things that you and do
My other humans who have you
Nor those that you have hurt too...

This is about Me
You cannot see what I can see
I will make you what I designed to be
God's yesterday word to me..

Me
Its not all about
He does love my shout
I know He's got the most clout
He says so and it is announced...

Yet
Some have not came to be
Still
To the message I cleave
I know and believe
This isn't and so is all about me...

The Lord's Promise

I've been hearing you call my name
Telling me with you I have all to gain
Lay your burdens at my feet. I'll take your pain
I am your King; with power and might I reign supreme
Cry to me for I am forgiving
Sins have been paid for
Let me heal your sores
Your heart, I promise to do my part
My word will not return void
It is more precious than gold
I could tell you of stories untold
The Lord promises I will give you your on beat
Your words are mine; so you will always speak
The Spirit makes musical notes fall from my lips
And the fire of God is coming from my fingertips
Let me tell you what the Lord says
All your children will speak in tongues and be saved
Even though I didn't want one
The Lord promised to send me a husband
I had let my heart be caused so much pain
I had to let him go when he came
He is not even in the same state as me
Still, I am patiently believing
My son who in prison is serving 30 years
The Lord says he will not stay there
The Lord showed me us writing a book together
From the point of the victim and the molester
I dream of hugging him when he comes home
I'm supposed to be seventy-two but I am not that old
God calls me Princess
I shall be filled with all the gifts
The Great Spirits' love is everything
Honest, loyal and forgiving
Compassionate, understanding and grace runs over
It says, “Don't look back. Your season is forward
If you stay, I will finish every thing I told you”
So I stay because I love what The Spirit do!

Nothing can separate me from this love on this planet
I got promises and I gotta have it!
No one on this earth can prove to me The Living God does not exist
It has saved my life to many times too prove it
The Lord says, “When you call, I'll answer. I'll move. I'll do it and know that I call you friend”
And I had let my mind believe The Lord didn't love me because of my sin
My Father says, “Don't be in doubt
What ever you need; I am looking out”
The King promises me a house and to repay nine years of trouble
I want that, need this on the double
So I wait. Sometimes not so patiently
But that's because with my whole heart: I believe
That the Great I Am will do all this for me
Providing me with wisdom, favor, healing and mercy
Faith is: knowing that which has not yet happened shall come to pass
I look forward to my future no longer living in my past
I must believe in God order to receive
I don't belong to anyone else to lead

The Heart of Me

Dear Lord bless us with something we didn't have before
Say there will be no more closed doors
Protect us from what's coming ahead
Shoo away evil before we get out of bed
Clear the wickedness
Fill us with your bliss
Love, peace and happiness
Give unto us your grace as You wish
Bestow upon us your Heavenly gifts
I stay on my knees praising Thee
Knowing how You coveted and covered me
Been my footprints in the sand
When man..wouldn't even hold my hand
Times I didn't know where I would sleep or eat
You loved me so deep
Gave me a bed and food in my belly
Where I would be without You, ain't no telling
All my life people been telling me You the one to turn too
And now I know this is true
You know all my issues
So I watch for what Your gonna do
Lord, You know my world
Where I been and where I'm going
Know my struggles and my pain
Your promises and my gain
So no mo playing, delaying
Disobeying the words I be saying
Calling on the mercy of the Lord
God please save my soul
Giving me the right to ask bold
The future You have foretold
Strength to walk my road
Til I reach the streets paved with silver and gold
To let go of all the negativity
Keep on with the positivity I need it like air and gravity
My life has not been one big tragedy
It has been the Master's planned strategy

Life has made me strong
Adversity made me hold on
I have a dream, a song to sing
My heart is with the Great I Am and the joy it brings

I Know I Belong to You

I lean on you I depend on what you do
I keep asking for little miracles
Not seeing that you are prehistorical
I have finally decided to let you give
Live the life you want me to live
I put all my faith in You
No man shall break through
With all your amazing grace
You keep me breathing everyday
When you call me home
I will never be alone
Won't be depressed, stressed
Can say goodbye to all this mess
But while I am still here
The point is very clear
No matter what I do
I belong to You
Even when I smoke, drink or get high
I still belong to the Spirit in the sky
Even when we are being wrong
Your loving is still so strong
Happiness does not come without pain
But through Him, we have all to gain
Every time I felt like I was on top
I never forgot You were my rock
On the days I felt, "Please, Lord, I can't take no more."
You created yet, another door.
When I feel I can't take another loss
I remember You paid the cost
Sincerely dearly, undoubtedly
Your always here for me
When I give my body so freely
You are the One who will never stop loving me
No matter how the doctor's say we are hurting
He is the One to close the final curtain
And while we keep striving
You keep providing

Even at times I feel threatened
I always feel Your blessings
When I cuss and fight
He is the owner of my life
He talks and walks with me every day
The only thing that is never out of place
We put our trust in people, jobs and money
When He is all that we should trust. Huh ain't life funny
He who gives everything
We take for granted. Indeed
Yet, He says, "I forgive them.
For we belong to him"
He loves us relentlessly, unconditionally
No matter what we are religiously
Forgiving us for all
Never letting go when we fall
If your living foul, no matter where your at
He has forgiven that
Let no man judge us where we stand
We all rest in God's hand
Even when you speak what you know is true
One day He will have judgment over you
That doesn't mean you won't make through those pearly gates
Remember every where we go we have a place
No one has a mercy like Him
And He gets the sweetest revenge
When the party is over and all is said and done
He is the one who sent His only begotten son
The sun, the sea, the earth, this world
Him, her, they and me. Everything is Yours

I Believe

I have promises from The King
Which I choose to believe
Heavenly gifts..I intend to receive
Talents to achieve my dreams
Faith in that which I cannot see
Love for you and me
Sensitivity fro everyone's needs
Passion to succeed
A Heavenly language to set me free
I have sewn my seeds
I wait in the Lord to reap
This is about me not you
I receive the word of truth
So if you have meanness, negativity
Please keep it to yourself
My heart relies on God not nobody else
My faith is not in mankind
If it was, I would lose my mind
I would live in bitterness, misery and fear
I had enough of that for far too many years
Shed so many tears
Words spoken to people who did not hear
Care shown to folks who did not care
God said, “I have always been there”
He who has never lied misused or abused me
I choose with my whole heart to believe

Lost Loved Ones

People say they are in a better place
You would rather they be in your face..

But remember them with a smile
If they were here for a short time or quite awhile..

They have merely left this ground
Listen closely..
You can still hear their sound..

They are still around
Even if not where you want them to be
Search where your eyes cannot see..

Lost loves may look for you spiritually
It has been told to me..

They cannot feel our sorrow
In a better place with no tomorrow..

Carried on the wings of angels
Where their bodies will never fail them..

Where pain cannot hurt 'em
Hearts will not break them..

Stress won't stress 'em
The enemy can no longer pursue them..

You see..
I do honestly believe in this place of Heavenly beings
Where my Father is the King..

Our lost loved ones..
We can't imagine what they are experiencing
So why your eyes are tearing..
Remember they are no longer fearing

Your grieving..they are not feeling..

You believe you'll never see them again. So much pain
Wondering how you haven't went insane..

STOP!!
They are still apart of your heart..

Take some time..give them so thought
Reminisce about the lesson they taught..

The food they cooked
How they smelled and looked..
Remember the smiles and laughs
It's not a thing of the past..

People say they are dead and gone
The spirit has simply moved on..

Probably singing the most beautiful song
Watching over their lost loved ones..

CHAPTER II
Loves of My Heart

I Am Me

43 years ago..a star was born
Found her voice and is about to sing her song
Loud and clear
For the whole world to hear
Lend her your ear
She can move you to tears
Help your pain to disappear
Put a smile on your face
Love you with grace
Be there in your time of need
I am her..and she is ME!-Momma Toya

The Truth

The truth will never look you in the eye
With a straight face tell a lie
The truth will never deceive you
Pack its bags and then leave you
The truth is not clever and charismatic
Say its got yo back and never had it
The truth is what it was
What it is and what it does
At the end of the day
The truth is not a lie no matter what you say

To My Family

God has something He wants me to tell you
And it must be true
Because I have always prayed for you
But now its some thing different
There's a groaning in my spirit
When the Lord speaks I can hear it
I can feel it and I believe it
No matter what eyes see
God shows me things differently
No matter what the world says
Each and every time I pray
God just gave me that
About to make it my facebook stat
To all my Bragg family
I pray for you constantly
Even if its been a long time since you have been seen
I have not forgot about your Being

Team Players

I wanna say "Thank you"
I'm still not cool
But I'm trudging thru
Thank you for whatever you did do
Some gave a place to live
Others gave all they had to give
Your kids kept my love active
Without joy I was still happy
You gave good advice
Loaned me money once or twice
Took the time for my son, to write
Your kindness constantly on my mind
I can feel your Sun rise
I'll be at the door with a surprise
Remembering how you helped my life
Wanting to return the smile
My team players, you know who you are
Didn't count me out like a falling star
Had my back when I didn't have it myself
I'm glad God sent you and no one else
I got love with all my heart
This first book is just a start
There are many more to come
Some of y'all will be around the world to see the sun
I'm not going to forget where I come from
Toledo, Ohio is my home. It's where I was born
Veda, Kiwania, Janell, Leonya
I'll never forget about ya
Cindy, Carla and Mary
My home Girls!! We so crazy
And to my number 1 Fan
Katrina (Carter) Bragg
I love my Baby Girl
The only one borne to me in this world
To Dominique, Timothy and Michael, my three sons
One day we gonna have some real fun
There are a lot more I haven't forgot, just didn't mention

When the time comes I'm gonna pay you some attention
Once again thank you to my team players
I'm not talking to the gossips, naysayers and haters
But don't worry, You got a poem coming to
This one right here doe, This ain't for you!

Loving You

Loving you seems like what I was born to do
Didn't know about you me and her too
Long time ago...You told me y'all was thru
How y'all kids went from two to three
Still some days seems to bother me..

Been so long since you been here
But I still feel yo sound in my ear
Yo touch on my waist
Your breath on my face
Let it go..back in the days
Oh, how my mind plays
We used to amaze
Drive each other crazy
Me..not knowing you already had a family..

See I was love sick. Had a Love Hangover
And just like Diana I don't want a cure
I was everything in between
Sweet and demure..

Opening my legs every time I opened the door
You wanna chill and conversation
I want chills and vibrations..

Remember the time you made me pull my hair out
Hokey-Poking, had me shaking all about
You put yo right foot in, Yo put yo left foot in
You put yo stick in and moved it all around
My cum came down and that's what I'm talking about...

I was the coolest chick you ever known
Off to Alaska I could have flown
Over the years my love was growing
So was yo family; but I'm not knowing...

But looking back: Late night dinners..I cooked

No clubs, no shows
No publicity, nobody knows..

About our all night, month long, years gone
Mind blowing SEX fest
Giving you my bestest
Hot spot been the wettest
It was; is missing you like a fetish
And year after year still a lil bit Co-co-coetish
Scared of the monster inside of you
Put that rod in my car and some more it grew..

Gotta a little bit harder to have you inside
You laughed at my pain; licked my tears when I cried..

I squint You moan; I squirm You groan
Just thinking about it got butterflies in my stomach
We both know when you in it; You own it
When you got it, You want it
Play with it, tease it and taunt it
I put this ass up in the air
While you is in there..

Stroking my emotions
While you rowing in this ocean
Waves of pleasure
Searching for my treasure
Sea of Love cuz
I'm thinking it's forever..

Ten years later I got a message in a bottle:
Gonna give this dick to you
Then too her tomorrow
That's just the way that it is
I'm not sorry for your sorrow...

You should have figured it out a long time ago
I'm the male version of a female ho
But it's not for you to take it personal

That's just the way it goes
Somebody cares and nobody knows

Away

Everyday I grow older
My love for you gets stronger
From sun up through sun down
No matter where your at your always around
Even when your not with me
You take my body to ecstasy
When you become a tease
I get low and nasty
If you were a hundred miles away
I would never miss your face
I think about you daily
Your soul reaches out and grabs me
Through all this space
My body still aches
You, you, you stimulate my mind
You handle me with a love that is so fine
Five minutes with you is like an hour or two
I'm so into loving what you do I do more for you
Every night is the night you get me right
And every morning there are noises of soul felt moaning
Anytime you say my name I hear
Even when your not here
The feel of your kiss
Lingers softly on my lips
You take me there
In the ways that you care
No other can find the place you got in my heart, body and mind
I rest in peace every night your next to me
And when your not
I fall asleep with my body still hot
No matter how long you are away
My love is here to stay
I won't deny it, not again
I will love you past my end
Just got to accept it
Your love got me infected
You conquer me to the center of my being

Making me feel ways I didn't know I was feeling
Five hours. Ten hours. To the twenty fourth power
I don't know of another love like ours
And I don't know of another beater like you
Plus you teasing it too
Fifteen hours. The day is brand new
Your hands are the key to unlock my doors
This is a feeling that can't be ignored
When your away of you I dream
I wake up outta my sleep and want you next to me
Right now your thinking about me too
And all the things we come to do
I feel you kissing and hugging, grabbing and tugging
Man I can't wait til I can give you this loving
You feel me scratching and rubbing, licking and sucking
I won't stop for nothing til my baby stop nuttin'
He knows he don't have to ask me twice
Love making always nasty and nice
Before I drift off to sleep
You're the happy thought that relaxes me
Twenty-four hours. Plus a day away
You're moving with me from place to place

Get On With It

My foot just can't feet these shoes
That are worn by a crew
Yeah it's obvious I'm gonna miss your kiss
The feel of it on my lips
I'm gonna miss those eyes that smile
You hitting it from the back for awhile
But you can get on with it
All this bull shittin
Lying
Conniving
This stuff I just ain't buyin

Sexing and sucking
The only thing got me striving
Inside of me my heart is dying
For real man my heart is dying
There's a pattern with us
I'm bout to change the design
No matter what you say or do
I'm not changing my mind
I'm saying this shit for the last fucking time
If you can't be all mine
Get on with it
Go be all you can be
Cuz I want a man who's dedicated to me only
See that's when your nights are never lonely

So you can get on with it
I'm not gonna deal with it
You can't tell me I'm the only girl
Who is sharing your world
I know I'm not the only one
feeling it cause I'm feeling it

This not the only toy box you're playing in
But you can't come back again and again
You keep saying you a street nigga

So I gotta say peace my nigga
Cause I know I'm a good woman
I don't have to check my figures
So I'm a get on with it
move along with it

Get me a man who wants to be committed
Find me one who loves to slide up in it
Saying No one compares to you girl
You got the best love in the world
And that mouth game
Will make a man's life change
I know your sex life will never be the same
When your alone in the dark
You'll wish you could say my name
But I done got on with it
Ain't no coming back to it
No matter how you try to hit me with that do it fluid
Boy you done blew it
I see the light and I'm running to it
Emerging on the other side
I can see clearer with my new eyes
Your just a man
Not part of the Master's plan
So I say goodbye to you
Go run yo streets and do you

I had to get on with it
I couldn't live with it
I'm a grown ass woman playing house
What's this all about?
I had to check myself
I'm pushing my love and it's been rejected
So I'm moving it along to one who wants to accept it

Cleaning out My Heart

Have you ever had a nigga lie 2 U again and again
I have so let me take U back to when my story begin
Back to 2000 when I thought I met an angel who walked among men
Didn't know I was trading my soul for a life full of sin...

Chilling, talking, sexing, having fun
Thinking he was the one
Well, I should have listened
I was too busy being tempted...

With the fine black body
I was teased and pleased
And the fruit you bared was so raw
I shouldn't have tried to take it so far...

Years later and I'm cleaning out my heart
The time came when we finally fell apart
Thoughts of you consuming my mind
And you were just passing time...

I gave my heart and soul
Only wanted to know you more
Still remember the last of you walking out my door
You don't know how I crumbled on the floor...

It took months for me to get back up
In limbo I was stuck
Then a friend came by
Reminded me that I was the prize...

I started cleaning out my heart
Took out all yo nasty parts
Living again. I was beginning to start
I had had to many bags to cart...

I had to tell it to my face
Besides me wasn't yo place

More like a waste of space
Cleaning my mouth of this bitter taste...

Oh and just so you know It was yo lies
That brought me to despise
If I knew your truth
I could have handled it Boo...

But you wanted to sneak and hide
In Toledo, a city only so wide
Tried yo best to keep me from yo family life
Yea you slipped it over on me once or twice...

But when I found out about the new baby
I went to your side of the closet and made it empty
And your standing there not even feeling guilty
Asking Why you wanna leave me...

Feelings are fleeting. My emotions are real
I never signed up for this deal
You didn't care how I would feel
But you knew I wanted our union sealed...

So I had some heart cleaning
Through a shine on it. Now I'm gleaming
No more memories screaming
Tear streaming...

No longer upset over what I thought was the best
Your just like the rest
Gave my body to you then you left
Unconscious about how I felt...

While I was cleaning up my heart I made a decision
Not just anybody could have that position
I remembered what the King said:
I'm gonna send you a husband...

In So Many Ways

In so many ways I trusted what you had to say
In so many ways I wanted us til the end of my days
In so many ways I'm missing you the further I move away
In so many ways there were reasons I wanted you to stay
In so many ways in you I could drift on the dock of the bay
In so many ways I loved your embrace
In so many ways my body, you would slay
In so many ways you took my mind to a different place
In so many ways I put my heart on display
In so many ways so much fun when we laid
In so many ways I never strayed
In so many ways I'm wondering why I got played
In so many ways why the egg on my face?
In so many ways I payed like I weighed
In so many ways each second I face I am brave
In so many ways watching the memories fade away

Wonder How You Are

I wonder how you are
State lines separate us so far
I still see you in my dreams
I wonder if your thinking of me..

I hear your voice loud and clear
I wonder if you want me near
Wonder how your love will sound in my ear..

Wonderful you are to meet
From everything I see
From the top of yo head to the soles of your feet
Wonder filled you are to me..

Wonder how yo breath smells in the morning
Wonder how you sound in the night when your moaning
I wonder how you spend your day
When you wanna play
I wonder what you say..

I wonder if I followed you
Where would you lead me to
I wonder if I lost it
Would you let me find my groove..

I wonder if you would hold me while I screamed
I wonder if in me You would believe
Wonder if you would help me with my dreams
Wonder if you and I together could succeed..

Wonder if I let you dive in
Could I be yours til the world's in
I wonder would you hold, accept, guide me
Say grow with me through eternity..
I wonder if we could cum together
Go with each other forever
I wonder if we could cry in the dark

Smile with the sun. Honestly I wonder if your the one..

Wonder if I could have love so true
It compels me to belong to you
Wonder if I could keep you for all time
I wonder if you will always be on my mind..

Missing Some You

I'm missing you so much
My mind still feels your touch
Your lips..so soft
Have no problems getting me off
Your head between my thighs
Makes me have to close my eyes
Kisses on the back of my neck
Make my inner parts wet
The feel of your hands on my body
Makes me moan..and cum softly
It's something about your member
That makes me gasp when you enter
I inhale a long breath
Then exhale til it ain't none left
Yo scent feels my nostrils
Your not here..still it's possible
I miss you more than I can explain
Hard to wait for you to make me cry your name
Hate to have to say I miss you so much
But waiting..is what I do..until I feel your touch

So in Love

I am in love..so in love and so glad to be there
I know my baby cares
Bout where I am at and what I be doing
And he ain't worried about who I be screwing
He know he got all this love
I know we are blessed from above
I am not threatened by any other girl
He makes me feel like the only one in the world
Says I'm The Lady In His Life
He the one I be with at night
In me, he sees the Godly light
He says it shines so bright
He knows I'm a good woman
By grace..I have been chosen
The Lord told me in '99 He would send a man
Back then I didn't accept the plan
I wanted my own wings to span
Not knowing I would obey the command
Between us things are easy breezy
I was given a promise and a dream
And in that I believe
I can hear the wedding bells ring
My heart has a love song to sing
Glad I didn't trust what I had seen
Instead, what a God said He would bring

My Love

You don't know about my love
How it gives and takes so much
How it grows without water
Contains all types of power
Last past the 28th hour
On the 9th day of the week
You can find me if you seek
I am near 367 days of the year
No matter how many times I shed so many tears
My heart could never be as cold as ice
Because my love is oh so nice
I step back a sec when I get upset
I'll be back again
Some thing like a best friend
I know about loving til the end
Even doe it has just began
The love I give to you
Is a part of my truth
Its like a tree that bears fruit
At 2 am My love will cook your food
My love will never go
Even if you ever want to say so
It is everlasting
Not time for passing
It's warm like Apple Pie
Visible in my eyes
More than strangers enjoying the night
Love Jones is quite alright
My love comes with respect
My love keeps my stanka dank attitude in check
Comes with passion
Enough fire to light a book of matches
To laugh louder at your jokes than every one else laughing
My love no one else is tapping
It is a happening
My love has actions
It is non-fiction

Not full of suspicions
Nor is it defensive
My love brings peace, fun and joy
It is for one man who was a very special little boy

Waiting

I've been waiting and I am waiting
Two different kinds loving and the hating..

I've waited for you to look her in the eye
Prepared to tell your lie..

Waited for you to ring my bell
Your secret little story you ain't gonna never tell..

Waited for you to leave in the morning
Didn't matter if I was still kinda horny..

I had been waiting for you to call again
Behind close doors we lovers in the open not even friends..

You involved me in a love affair
Took years for me to even be aware..

Trusted you before anything
Didn't see the lies you were weaving..

Then I waited because you said you was leaving
Now I was the one being deceived..

Finally I didn't want to wait no more
So I packed yo stuff and met you at the door..

Waiting for the Lord to heal my heart
I prayed for the one who would never depart..

The one who has patience and understanding
Everlasting fire to ignite my passion..

Wisdom to value my vision
Insight to trust my decisions..

Smarts with a brain like mine

Love in a heart so kind..

One who believes in loyalty
Be faithful and adore me..

I cried, screamed, prayed and waited
Trusted in the Lord to answer my prayers..

And then I waited...

And I waited some more
Then the Lord brought me to his door..

But wait because I still have too
He was everything the Lord said He would do..

But he like me has trust issues
Out of life experiences they grew..

He shared so much with me
Parts of his inner being..

But he did not chose to share his life
To make me his wife..

So I left running out of patience
But I'm not gone just still waiting..

For the love to stop hurting
And the mind to stop wondering..

And God to begin the healing
The messes to end in which we're dealing..

I wait for his smile, voice, touch again
I know he's gonna be my best friend..

Love me like no other
So cliché but we will always be together..

Waiting in love for love
Dreams keep me reminiscent of..

I am waiting for the one who supports and cares
The thoughtful one who will always be there..

Whose heart and mind
Are only mine til the end of time..

A good old fashioned possession obsession
A union blessed from heaven..

I don't mind waiting
Ya dig what I'm saying..

My love is to worthy
Believe me Babe I ain't in no hurry...

My BFF

My BFF Forever, let me down, never
Lie to me? Rather die for me
Keeps it real. No other way to be
No broken promises. On some honor shit
Never quit. My Nigga 2 legit
Through all my heartbreaks
U never changed
My BFF til our end
We like lions in the den

So protective of my body
Even when I shared it with every body
Mended my heart
When I let some other tear it apart
Feeds my mind with soul food
And its all good
Saved my soul with prayers
Said to hell with the naysayers

My best friend in the background
Always around
Fun times going down
Meeting up in T-Town
20 years strong and we have clowned
My Nigga never judged me
Always stood up for T

Our friendship is very special
It don't contain the elements of evil
We are concerned about our dreams and losses
Both of us wanting to be bosses
We go back to rims on a Cadillac
It was a blue one wasn't it Fat Daddy

Bye Bye Haters

Back in the days we had Goodie Mob telling us we had Beautiful Skin
Now rappers trying to get you to give up the skins
So many single mothers raising so many kids
Most men are takers no longer giving
Smash your friends yo sister and your mother
Some cats will even tap yo brother
Some are more fighters than lovers
No more positive role models
Then ya family the first to see you in the gutter
Step over you and go help another
Talking about you behind your back
So far from stating the facts
I don't have to accept acts
I know how to close my eyes and turn my back
I know how to tell and face the truth
Don't lie like niggas in the booth
My heart can play many roles
But I don't have to do what you say so
You know me but you don't
Cuz if you did you wouldn't front
Having a love hate relationship with maturity and respect
Because the old me wants to get in wreck
The now me says keep it in check
The best ain't over with yet
I gotta get up, get out and do something
The 90's rappers was really saying something
People act like 70's music kinda funky
Get off my back you damned monkey
Trying to get me for my money
Don't let the sweetness fool you, honey
It's best for me to roll out
Don't need to be no where near your mouth
Bout to head back South
Where they know what real love is about
Its in fun when we scream and shout
Ain't nobody trying to detour your route
Honesty and loyalty be the best to me

Mix in some compassion, understanding and sympathy
We know how to be friends for sho
Come to Ohio. To the T-O-L-E-D-O
She ain't got a bed then yo home girl will let you sleep on the floor
No need to be worried about locked doors
I really ain't gotta say no more
Except some people don't love from their core

Hope

I have pain from people kids dying in the street
Some are even babies in their cribs still sleep..

Young nigga you wanna pick up a gun?
Join the Army-get your serve on..

Everybody complain about the government
Were the ones who did or did not vote for them..

Still your the ones causing war on yo street
With some silly ass beef..

They in their mansions watching the news
Look at these niggas “They some damn fools”..

I betcha Martin and Rosa crying in their graves
Knowing they stuck together more when they were slaves..

More freedom than its ever been
But Black Boys can't all grow up to be Black Men..

What the hell was the Freedom Riders fighting for?
Kids can't sleep peacefully in they beds no mo..

Instead of the white man coming to lynch 'em
It's them stray bullets coming to get them..

And you say you got a reason
Ain't enough of one for the killing season..

All y’all fools should be jailed for treason
Killing off our own people..
The whole city know about family tragedy
Are you seriously kidding me?..

People dying over bullying
Man that's senseless insane to me

Grown men claiming blocks
So you can tear it down to start selling rocks

Don't know nothing about building
Do you understand about how you be feeling?..

I wish most of y'all would take an initiative
Start teaching these kids

Of another life to live
You have so much more to give

You can be healers, teachers
Helpful and community leaders

You don't have to be gang bangers, thieves or selling dope
Put down the guns and pick up Hope

What? You scared? We live in a war zone
Some of y'all mothers fear you won't make it home

Who wants to get shot and die in the streets?
Food For Thought. "Aye baby, Give these fools something to eat"

How many of y'all can count ten friends in the grave
It never occurred that they made you the modern day slave?

Man Listen...I'm not never gonna stop preaching
Somewhere my words are reaching

Use your heart and your mind
To do something other than crime

Love on some body, clean up your neighborhood
Buy some food, walk yo kids home from school

Helps somebody move they couch, go paint a house
Speak words of Wisdom out cha mouth

I'm just saying there is some thing else you can do
Before your one less body in your crew

Good thanks for the future Race
One day I hope our lives will never be the same

Just Me

I am not pro or con anything
I love and respect Human Beings
I don't discriminate
To me that is hate
I am not a Creator
Don't know where you go later
But while I am around
I want smiles
Good memories
Participation in my daily dreams
If you hate me because I am black
I cannot change that fact
Because I am short, fat with natural hair
Go tell somebody who cares
If you dislike me because I have missing teeth
You don't even have to talk to me
I'm broke still in the hood eating pork
Full of encouragement and hope
My life ain't no joke
Cried enough tears to make me choke
Still I achieved my growth
Have a sense of my worth
I don't care what you prefer
I won't hurt you with my words
That's not what I'm here for
If you choose to bring the pain
I'm not going to go insane
I know how to close the door
And not deal with you no more
Without being mean, screaming obscenities
Who you are won't stop me from being me

Fallen

To all the fallen hero's sons and daughters
The many who go down in the slaughter..

Mothers and fathers. Sisters and brothers
The best of the fallen soldiers..

The ones who went to war prepared to die defending a country
And those that died representing they streets..

Doing what you feel you gotta do
So many left behind to miss you..

Crying to the Lord its not fair
Why can't they be here..

Hard to close their eyes at night
Wondering if everything will ever be alright..

What do you tell your children
About the victims of the system..

Would they even care of the reason why
The ones they love cannot be there to say goodnight..

Whoever made murder okay
How many lives can you take today..

The death of any human being is inhumane
To kill for personal gain to me is just insane..

But for those of you who feel like you do what you gotta do
I raise my hand and salute you..

I am glad your choice is not mine to make
A soul is not for me to take..

Whether on the battlefield of war or the battlefield of the mind
Someone might just have left before their time..

So for our fallen friends take a moment to remember them
Transparent with love no judgment..

Forget the body that perished
The good, the bad, the ugly that's what we cherish..

Untitled

I don't mind helping out I despised getting used
I love having friends but fake ones ain't cool
If you care enough to talk behind my back
Keep it like that
If I say I love you believe its true
No matter what you say or do
I may say angry words when I get upset
Not gonna play you doe this you can bet
Lie, steal or curse you out
Not what I'm about
I accept those for whoever they are
But don't won't to get hurt by far
If you turn yo back on me, I know how to turn mine too
If you extend your hand I know how to hold yours too
If you can listen to my problems
I can be yo shoulder to cry on
If you feed me when I'm hungry
I got you when your thirsty
I'm about give and take
We all need help with or without mistakes
If you on my front line
I got yo backside
If you don't show me some love
You gets no lovin' babe
I wear my heart on my sleeve
When it gets cut then I bleed
God and I patch it back together
Then its like whatever
Stormy Weather thru you..I pray
I feel differently in my day
No longer justified by my pride
Tears slowing up from my eyes
One day I will learn to turn the other cheek
When God finishes off the human nature of me
I'm assuming I won't hurt at all
A life promise form God is worth my Heavenly call

CHAPTER III
Freaky Tails

Married to My Mouth

He married to my mouth
Always in it when the lights go out
He loves my lips
With this soft touch grip
Tip of my tongue
Gotta a nigga sprung
With my teeth I bite his meat
Touch my tonsils when I deep throat
He shakes when I gag and choke
My fingers, like circles, intertwined
Day and night on his mind
Thoughts of me 24/7
His private Heaven
Hot as hell
Ice always melting
Whole body sweating
From all the nuts I'm catching
Forget catching my breath: I'll just be breathless
With this sweet treat in my mouth
On my knees in front of the couch
Nibble on it like an ear of corn
No teeth marks when I'm done

Best Friend

I done really only had sight or two
So I don't know why I'm dreaming of you
I feel you touching me, rubbing me
feeling me sucking me
Nothing like a tease
More like the guy of my dreams...

Somehow I spend the day with you
Your kids and your crew
Riding around T-Town and I'm your Boo
Dressed alike. We so cute
Getting some thing to eat
Visiting yo peeps...

I woke up from the dream
He. Not you. Was laying next to me
What would he do
If he knew I was thinking of you
He, you and I
Oh what a night..

Get up fix breakfast for me and him
Already can't wait to get to sleep again
Moving about in a haze
Laughing with him. Wondering...

Finally, happily back to sleep
Off to dream world of you and me
Oooohh, kissing. I like this
Lips so soft covering my mouth
Fingers gripping my hair
You're his best friend and we don't care...

I love the smile on yo face
Right before you taste my sweet place
And when you over my face

Giving me the best beating I've ever had
In between all of that...

Letting you hear
When I moan, groan and bite your ear
I show you when I start shedding tears
You feel me when my body starts convulsing
Bursting like Fourth of July explosions...

I'm still trying to remember how to breathe
Some body is entering me
It is the one I want to be my man
D-A-M-N
Whispering your so wet
I smile silently thinking 'Yo best friend did that'
My mind is screaming from excitement
We made love in the quiet
Cuz saying his name
Could not be explained
As my heart and body ached for him
I laid calmly up under his best friend

Love Master

What do you call it when he knows your body inside and out
Every time you see him makes you wanna let your panties drop
Feel butterfly kisses on both ya lips
Do the side of your neck
Purple passion marks on your breast
Whenever your horny He got an 'S' on his chest
And a hard time to match
What's his name? I call him the Love Master
Every time he run up in you
He knows exactly what to do
He knows what he's after
Orgasms on top of orgasms
Soft moans, low groans
He says the sound of your voice really turns him on
And you love the way he twist his wrist
When he got his fingers up in it
Nails scratching yo leg, tongue on your thigh
You can't stop the tears from your eyes
Closed so tight
This a new kind of hype
The Love Master lays you across his lap and masturbates you
Brings you to ecstasy for an hour or two
Like he kidnapped your body but got you begging for more
Every sound, move, he adores
And when it comes to the head you can't even handle that
He got you walking around with a permanent arch in your back
That's why he's called a Love Master
Still cumming the morning after
Seven, eight more orgasms
Somebody is laughing
It gets kinda hard to breathe
Your thinking what is he doing to me
Hot hands all ova you to help you relax
Yes the Love Master even does that
Comforting
With sensuality

He rest while you take a ride
And he looks so good you won't close your eyes
He starts going insane
Pulling your hair and saying your name
Since this is such a poker game
The Love Master goes for change
Puts you on your back
Spreads the legs from here to Iraq
Nipples being softly bitten
Body being hard driven
Up under his rhythm
Mind goes blank body goes limp
So much cream between the sheets
Hot box letting off rocket ship heat
Girls, with a Love Master ain't nothing but fun
So call one up whenever you wanna cum

What I Want

You excite me, thrill me
Soothe my soul, groove me
I want you to take my hand to hold. Be my friend
There is no end
I want to feel your essence
Put my head on your chest and sink in
What you know about that?
I think of you and get purrs from my cat
Waiting to suck you dry and rub yo back
My body sears with heat without any actions
Touch me and my body like a reactor exploding
Something like yo balls when I be licking and holding
Busting nuts
I can feel in my guts
Making me love it
Cumming so thick
You do more than make my heart race
Make me shake and quake
Getting up with you is better than a wake and bake
I gotta express my feeling
Your the only man with whom I'm dealing
I wanna get to know you better
Not cuz of yo looks or cheddar
It's the things that I know
That make me wanna know you mo
Hafta admit I wanna love you slow
Enjoy your mind, go with your flow
I can wait patiently, understanding
To see you walk naked in our mansion
But if we don't have a chance
I can walk away without a second glance
Think of you from time to time
Til thoughts of you float out of my mind..

Addiction

He addicted to this deep throat
I'm addicted to his long stroke
Just the right pressure when he chokes
My body go limp when I squirt
I'm wetter than the Niagara
He growing like he on Viagra
Biting my lip so I won't scream
He stops. All over him I cream
Ooomph, ooomph, ooomph he says
Pulls me to the end of the bed
Spread my legs up in the air
My wetness
Wettin' both of us
He put the tip
In my passion pit
Slowly. Moving it in and out
Rubbing on my G-spot
I moan, I whine
He's go deeper than time
I cry. Pain is pleasure
“Please daddy make it last forever”
“Be quiet. Don't talk”
Up in my body like he doing The Walk
I gripped the bed, pull my hair, suck my fingers
As the last of the last orgasm lingers
He loves when I act like that
He always got his Ackrite together
Walking in the stormiest weather
Never let a little rain
Stop him from making me go insane
Now I lay on my stomach. Wrap my legs around his waist
Stare in the mirror so he can see the looks on my face
I watch him smile, roll his eyes
As he feels nuts 21, 22, 23, 24, 25
He goes to put it in my butt
I say “Nooo”. He says, “Shut up”

Pushes it slowly all the way in
Lays on my body as nut 26 begins
Enjoying how I squirm and tremble
He start beating my ass up like he Kimble
Hand around my waist
Holding me in his place
The other on my neck, biting on my shoulder
Making it hurt so good I don't want it to be over
Not with nut 30 around the corner
I arch my back, fuck him back
He the only one who get it like that
Serving that dick like it's made of crack
I'm almost done
Can't take no more nut 31
Weakly I say his name.
He covers my mouth
I feel him yea its rocked
I He puts fingers in my mouth to make me shut up
So I suck and deeper he thrust
Before I have a word to say
He puts a pillow over my face
And does it faster
Got me screaming oh God like I'm a pastor
Feeling like I walked across desert land
Drinking a bag of sand
I hoarsely say his name
"Yes, Baby"
"You ready to cum"
"Yes, Baby"
I say his name, murmur it, whine it, cry it
He like a piece of steel
But he's losing his will
All that suave ass composure: over
No control to gain
Say my name
"LA..TO..YA.."
Now he's whining, crying
I'm doing all the grinding
He paralyzed. Feet stuck to the floor

Talking about “Don't move”
Too late daddy I'm in my groove
I wiggle my hips
His backbone slips
He on his tippy toes bouncing the stick
Get it I start to think
I'm bout to cum he moans in my ear
Go head baby Give it here

Body Calls

Calling you..its my body
Saying I like what you do to me
Yo motion in this ocean
Got emotions overflowing
So much love you never knowing
Going half crazy cuz I can't just be showing
The thoughts in my mind constantly growing
When you slide between my thighs
And I close my eyes
No longer in the bed simply paradise..

When you bite my lips
I fight back the tears
Afraid they'll reveal just how I feel
Listen to my body talk, Baby
Some times words get in the way
All this hotness, wetness, telling you something
I wanna be yo baby, girl wife or sumthen
I don't be cumming like that for nothing
Wrap my legs around you and lightly scratch yo back
Feels so good I wanna stay like that
You don't know how hard it is to compose my act..

The way you push inside and flick your tongue
Got me cumming and going
Boy I stay on the run
The size of your mannishness feels me up
With me as your girl. I'll keep you built up
Never tear you down. You'll wanna keep me around
Listen to my body as it talks with sounds
Even when your not here
Its got something it wants you to hear
You make it throb and quake, wake and bake
Keep my body with a lot to say

Do Me Baby

I need a man who will go all the places his mind can go
It can feel every gap, every hole
Even go between my toes...

You give me some thing I can feel
I I'll suck the back of yo heel
Ride you in a Glass House
Give the people something to talk about...

What I want is some kissing and some hugging
It's like good music: keeps my ears buzzing
Some hands all over me
Teasing and Pleasing...

Passion makes me so so wet wet
Pulling my hair, pushing it there
Kissing the back of my neck
Causing me to melt...

I put my lips on it and it gets a lil bigger
First time in yo life I'm a good licker
You don't understand my flicker
You bust quit like Niggas pulling triggers...

You stay hard since you like me so much
So now I'm bout to feel you up in my guts
Later you gonna wanna touch me in my butt...

I love the change of color in yo eyes
When we slip and slide
And you touching my sides
With the slow motion grind...

Just like oil I'm so slick
The cum from me rejuvenates your stick
You touch me long time and I'm loving it

No need for spit and I really don't like that shit...

You lay your body on my back
And lick my ass crack
How do you think of stuff like that?
Got yo face up in when you start to smack…

Hard as a rock
A new G-Spot
Pushing inside deeper and deeper
Got me so hot as if I got a fever
Temperature rises
He scratching my thighs
I love when he do me like that so I roll my eyes...

Oh, what a mess I make
When my body shakes
Moving all over the place...

Because we do nasty disgusting shit
He goes right back and kiss my lips
Once again I like getting done like this
I make a grab for it...

Then he does this swirly thing with his tongue
He got me on the run
Screaming. Pulling his hair
And if his neighbors heard; you know I don't even care...

I Keep Him Coming

I keep him coming baby, everyday
Monday straight thru til Sunday
He be coming baby, in all ways
He keep cumming with me always...

Every morning before he take that morning piss
I slide his piece between my lips
Sleep still in his eyes
He enjoys his daily morning surprise
Now that that's finished
I get up and make our breakfast...

He takes a piss and brush his teeth
Greets me with my morning kiss..so happy
We eat and discuss our day
For the next eight hours we go our separate ways
Just before dinner
He'll be cumming again...

I keep him coming baby, Everyday
Monday straight thru til Sunday
He be coming baby in all ways
He keep cumming with me always...

Now his work day is done
Time for his baby to give him some fun
Come in and I'll take off your shoes
Man..I love catering to you
For your back rubs I warm up the oil
I keep my baby oh so spoiled...

Willing and able to give you good lovin'
Love to keep my baby cumming and humming
Rubbing on your thighs looking in your eyes
Waiting on the rush of Vanilla Sunshine
You sitting on the couch on swell in my mouth

Knowing I go all out every time I go down South...

I keep him coming baby everyday
Monday straight thru til Sunday
He be coming baby in all ways
He keep cumming with me baby always...

The day is done. Time to go to bed
I love how you keep me cumming when your giving me head
Split my lips with your tongue tips
Fill my ocean before you take a dip...
Slide your finger in to test the water
Like a sauna its getting hotter and hotter...

You stop. Climb on top of me
Push inside. Going all the way deep
Look into my eyes. Hold it there a sec
Because you love that it leaves me breathless
Your surrounded by my wetness
Always coming to get this...

I keep him coming baby everyday
Monday straight thru til Sunday
He be coming baby in all ways
He keep cumming with me always...

You Groove Me

You are something like a 90's beats
Night and Day I love when you Come and Talk To Me..

Oh, To Be Alone With You Groove Is In The Heart
They could Never Tear Us Apart..

More than Feenin' when I ride that Pony
You Give Me The World cuz I'm so Horny..

My Doggie Style makes you Smile
Yo Nasty Grind has me Slow Wind..

12 Play with Peaches and Cream
I Don't Want To Be A Player No More Your All That I Need..

Come Up To My Room and I'll make you Confess
"Your Love Is The Best"..

Cusswords..just let 'em roll
But remember my body Just A Lil Too Short..

A few Cocktails, them some Freaky Tales
And we can go Back To The Hotel..

You can call me Bitch
Butcha better say it like that Nigga from Oakland did..

No Vaseline need be applied
Make It Rough and spread these thighs..

I Need To Be owned by you
Hope your happy to Give Me You..

Feels So Good to have Love On My Mind
I feel like Sarah when she smiles..

Please Don't Go This IS My Heart
I Wanna Sex You Up and make you say Uhh Ahh..

You'll never have to call Tyrone
You Got Me. My love goes On & On..

There is no End of The Road
Not Another Sad Love Song..

Never Keeping Secrets And Our Feelings won't be missing
For The Cool In You is more than Illusions..

Something In Your Eyes showed me
You were a man with Sensitivity..

Just Like Daddy you take care of me
You more than want me Only When Your Lonely..

Don't Let Go (Love). You have me So Anxious
I will love you As (Always) til the earth becomes ancient..

Game Boy

Defender of my heart no Family Feud
Never crude or rude always so cool
But if he come under heavy fire
He'll attack back like Contra
Spray you with the Chrono Trigger
Mortal Kombat so Tetris nigga
Not a Street Fighter but he'll go hard on Xmen
I won the Wheel of Fortune
Do anything he want me to do
Even go Duck Hunting
Never ever left me in Jeopardy
So glad your my Final Fantasy
Centipede all up in me
Got my feeling like a Princess
When you go Sonic, Donkey Kong
All up on it
I call you Mr. Pac Man,
Boy you got a kick stand
Racing me like F-Zero
You my Guitar Hero
I Shake, Rattle and Roll
Got me on Adventure Island
Calling me your Night Rider
Biting on my neck like yes Castlevania
No more Pitfalls
He my Superman he got it all
Barbie dream boat, car and house
When its Burger Time
Lean steaks in our mouth
I'm treated like a Phantasy Star
Blessed by the heavens we are
Your my Super Smash Bother
Don't want another lover

Let's Play

Like a pitcher stepping up to bat
You break a sweat
I arch my back like nigga get off me
Neva that. I want to Slide with you thru eternity
Swing after swing getting all of this
Feels like I'm getting Hit
He's a Slugger at the Mound getting ready for a Grand Slam
If he can't do it no one can
All the Bases Are Loaded
Rounding Home for a big explosion
I feel every Long Stroke before its coming
A lil bit further and I'll be cumming
When he hit the Rough he know how to handle it
Got a girl screaming "Damn Daddy. Shit"
He Driving it home
I squirm and moan
He hit it hard off the Tee
Feeling every part of me
We wrestle in the bed
An arm under yo leg, a hand over my head
He Bust Open making a Cheap Shot
He got a Clean Finish cuz he made me Drop
He's the Enforcer with his Five Moves of Doom
I'm Gassed while I'm Gushing
The Ring General steady pushing
Got a good Screwjob with a Signature Move
Getting his Swerve on with the Beat Down groove

Now he's gonna need an Assist to get the Backdoor Play
Back Court in full effect no Fast Break
Flagrant Fouls not allowed
You need to take that back Downtown
No Double Dribble
Getting my ass is not so liberal
Don't end up in a Penalty Situation
You betta make this a smooth Transition

Although I do have a Weak Side
So if you Tip In we might go to Overtime
Now I'm Down By Contact
He Half The Distance to my Gap
During Hang Time my Hands To The Face
He wants a quick Score so he uses Dive Play
I gotta call an Audible
Cuz this Blitz is intolerable
Leading With The Head finding a Pocket
Immediately turns me into a Slobberknocker
Got my legs split like a Wishbone
Immaculate Reception, My baby headed to the Zone
Downhill Runner. Your my number one stunner
Quick Snap and I'm in the Sack. Never no Fumble
I like being on your team and your a good coach
When ever we play we both be winning the most
I'm ya Star Player. A real Good Sport. The MVP
I own the Heisman Trophy
We are World Series Champions
I stay in the Master's Tournament
You the all time Slammy Award Winner
We veterans ain't no beginners
You love playing hard with me
The day I die you'll Retire My Jersey

~Notes~

Royalty Publishing USA™
What's Your Story?
www.royaltypublisingusa.com
1 866 336 0001

~Gratitude~

I am grateful for every one who has ever encouraged me to pursue my dream, living or passed on. I want to give a very special thanks to Tiashaun Moran Brown, My sister who walked every road with me. To my brothers David and Lamar who listened to almost every poem I ever wrote. My sister Tamika Foster who fed me fabulously. My brother Michael Bragg who kept me rolling in more ways than one. And my brother Vernon Brinkley Jr when I was younger I wanted to get rich so I could come see you; writing was the only way I could think of. I love you people.

www.ingramcontent.com/pod-product-compliance
Ingram Content Group UK Ltd.
Pitfield, Milton Keynes, MK11 3LW, UK
UKHW040558210726
13854UKWH00008B/1488

9 781329 718463